Think in the Now
For Success

Feel Better - Do Better Staffing & Consulting

Maximizing Potential

Nonfiction/Self-Help/Business/Career

Think in the Now
For Success

by
Izzy Isidora Lewis

Edited by **Armani Valentino, Izzy Lewis &Tanya Terry**

Cover Design by Phillip Dannel & Armani Valentino

TABLE OF CONTENTS

Dear Reader,

This book was written with you in mind. Sometimes in life our experiences are for us, and other times theyare to help someone else in the future.

First, our grand entrance introduces us to the world: BIRTH. After birth, we enter infant stage, leading to adulthood. Living our adult life is that time in our lives that we face our most challenging moments.

Most of us struggle with making decisions, being motivated, living a successful life, as well as being confident in our daily decision-making approach.

Think in the now. We often allow the stresses of life and the fear of the unknown to determine our today thinking. This book will give you insights and steps to take to "Think IN the Now."

Izzy Lewis

INTRODUCTION

What Inspired Me To Write This Manual?

For as far back as I can recall I always had questions. I recall asking about a neighbor at the age of 3, while on my way to Pre-School. My question was deep, analytical and investigative. I asked my parents about the (neighbor's) lady's husband. Then, I asked my mom why is it that a different partner is there with her at different moments; (this was the next door neighbor) this was my observation. Of course I did not realize that those skills and awareness were molding my THINKING abilities and my ability to THINK IN THE NOW.

I am sure, at that moment, all my parents wanted to do was to shut me up, and therefore, told me, "Mind your own business." To date when my mom gives me compliments and reminds me of my strengths, she references that story. She reassures me that she knew very early that I would be who I am and that she needed to put me to school quick and fast to expand on those qualities. Thanks, Mom, Florine Doris for believing in me, even when I did not understand the details.

I wrote this manual. Why? Though in the moment of your thinking, in the moment of your experiences and your confusion, an answer may be missing, there is hope, KEEP THINKING. Not having an answer does not substitute for ending your thinking and your curiosity. Thinking is what leads us to concrete achievements. Through thinking, we learn new information about ourselves, we realize what truly matters to us, and we become aware of those things that we know, those things that we do not know.

I recognized my strengths early but did not know how to develop them. I recognized at the age of 13 that I was a keen listener. I realized that others could easily trust me. I also realized that I am a leader.

How did I realize that I was a keen listener? I wasable to listen to my family members, specifically mymother. I was able to empathize with her, yet not immediately have a solution for her concerns.

I owned my title as a LEADER when I applied formy first job at the age of 15 years, saved money to take a vacation yearly; though it was only $100. I owned being aLEADER. When I was able to convince "every day"friends to do what I asked (delegated), by setting up pro- jects and goals, I knew I was a leader. I recall leading the project of pooling our resources to buy our first car at 17 years of age without our parents' help. I owned being a leader from early when I recognized my strengths and myweaknesses. At that time, I was unaware of the terms strengths and weakness. All I knew was what worked andwhat did not work. In recognizing what works, you can increase those positive mannerisms. By knowing what does not work, you can visit the "Why?" zone. You are also able to search and ask for help; to decrease those things that do not work (better expressed as WEAK-NESSES).

I also recognized early at the age of 16 that I was agood Negotiator. Today, I am a Certified Mediator through Southern Methodist University; assisting individuals in reaching an agreement in their everyday lives. How did I recognize that talent? In my teenage years, closer to the time of graduating high school and preparing to go off to College, I negotiated with my parents for everything. If my parents expressed that I could not at- tend a school event, I would set up a meeting with them to discuss their decisions and question their reasoning. I also did this to reassure them of my strong morals and values. Again, my mother specifically would say: "None of my children are like you, I am not sure where you came from." She meant "You are surely different, but I welcome your approach!"

After being married at 22 to a man who is 12 yearsmy senior, I pushed on negotiating myself through the marriage. I took no shame in bargaining. I bargained for putting off having children to accomplish a Master's Degree. I bargained bank accounts, as well as spendingequality (that was fun). Thank you, George, for making me stronger and assisting in developing my strengths.

Though I knew most of my strengths, I did not know where to go or who to go to, to increase those positive characteristics (better described as STRENGTHS). Where did I get stuck? In the past, because my parents and siblings did not know the answers to my question, nor were they interested in being a resource, I got stuck.

This manual was created to expand your thinking. If you're thinking, Where can I find the answer when my parents do not know? When my older sibling has noclue? When I did not, learn all the details in school? What do I do and how do I remain positive and encouraged?

Fast-Forward

Let us fast-forward. I always knew that I wanted to achieve a formal collegiate education. However, what I did not realize is how difficult it was going to be to find the support and encouragement; especially when I was the first in my family to go as far as achieving Master's Degree.

I had to learn how to speak to MY INSIDE. When no one had the answers or was unable to help me maximize my potential, I was stuck again. Why was I stuck? I knew what I liked; working with others and helping others. I knew what I was good at; I was good at setting goals and AIMING high. What I did not know, that took me five years to learn is how to be resourceful, and this is one reason I was stuck. Also, I did not know how to build great relationships that may later be a RESOURCE to tap into when I was unsure or had doubt. I had no MENTORS.

I learned how not be discouraged. I learned that I would fail at times! I learned that though an MBA was not the end of my LEARNING, it paved the way for my thinking and gave me those skills to manage my own business. While going through life's challenges, at times it feels as though you are not making progress. ALL the failures, all those steps and redirections mold YOURTHINKING and allow you to think your way into SUCCESS.

Think in the Now
For Success

CHAPTER 1

Past Approaches & Experiences

Feel Better - Do Better Staffing & Consulting
Maximizing Potential

Past Approaches & Experiences

Let us take two to five minutes and reflect on our lives from young adult age to current age. Do you think you had struggles completing high school? Do you thinkabout the struggles you had staying motivated and pre- paring for college? Do you recall how great it was when mom and dad said they would pay for college?

PAST EXPERIENCES

What struggles did you have from age 13- 18?

_____

_____

_____

_____

_____

_____

_____

List moments/situations when you struggled with motivation, confidence and security in your choice and decisions.

_____

_____

_____

_____

_____

_____

_____

Think in the Now for Success

List three of your most scary and difficult financial challenges between the age of 15- 23.

1._____
_____
_____
_____
_____
_____
_____

2._____
_____
_____
_____
_____
_____
_____

3._____
_____
_____
_____
_____
_____

Past Approaches & Experiences

YOUR PAST APPROACH

Often times, when we look back at how we dealt withour past, it gives us insight into how to live better TODAY. In conquering our fears, accepting our weak- nesses, and learning from our environment, we often live better today than we did yesterday.

List three memorable experiences you have had that mold and shaped your present life.

1._____

_____

_____

_____

_____

_____

2._____

_____

_____

_____

_____

_____

3._____

_____

_____

_____

Think In The Now For Success

Name three of your most memorable influencers in making decisions; such as mentors, teachers, and/or societal leaders and icons.

1._____

_____

_____

_____

_____

_____

_____

2._____

_____

_____

_____

_____

_____

_____

3._____

_____

_____

_____

_____

_____

_____

Past Approaches & Experiences

When we visit our Past Experiences and our Past Approach we should be able to learn from our experiences and build on our approach. Many times we meet people along the way of our journey that mold our thinking and give us a moment of "now I know better." With these simple ways of thinking and attitude of gratefulness, we are able to live for today and THINK IN THE NOW.

CHAPTER 2

Educational Investment

Educational Investment

When we think of education and investing in our future, we are quick to think about the "fear and hesitation of the unknown."

Education is much more than being enrolled in the formal system known as college. It is being conscious of the need to learn both inside and outside the traditional classroom. If nothing else teaches you, life will.

We are educating ourselves when we:

(a) Admit that no one is perfect, and there is a purpose for each of us on Earth.

(b) Take notes from a great conversation with a men-tor, parent, or person of influence.

(c) Read books and follow someone who captures our interests and attention in the direction of our career in-terests or personal life interests.

(d) Admit that we do not know everything and that we are open to new knowledge and approach.

NO ONE IS PERFECT

Every moment that you encourage yourself and think positively, you are educating yourself. Each time you listen in to something that you have never heard or known of, you are educating yourself. Each time you recall a past advice or experience that you regret you are educating yourself.

Think in the Now for Success

What you do with your thoughts is what is important. Taking your thoughts to the next level is what will allowyou to "think in the now" and "live in the now." So, how do you take your thoughts to the next level?

You take your "self-education" up a level by increasing your thoughts. Those thoughts become words; your words become ideas; your ideas become goals; your goals become your SUCCESSES.

TAKE NOTES

Why should you take notes from life's lessons such as seminars, a conversation with grandma/grandpa, or eventhe evening news? You take notes because your brain will not be able to remember all that you have encountered. Taking notes helps you be able to brainstorm or reflect on the information. You take notes, for future use to help you in certain situations, to reach your goals,and to have ease in your everyday activities.

Notes are often useful information even after years of an encounter. After 72 hours of hearing information, the majority of what we heard is not remembered. Much like trying to remember the phone numbers of everyone you meet at an event, it is better to collect business cards versus trying to remember every name, email ad- dress, and phone number. It is important to store the in-

formation in a reliable place such as legal pads, journals, computer files or other personal choices that are convenient and reachable for your reference.

Name (3) three specific sources from which you wouldtake notes (e.g. reading a book, a conversation with a mentor, or a conversation with a teacher):

1._____

_____

_____

2._____

_____

_____

3._____

_____

_____

READ BOOKS-AUDIO BOOKS-VIDEOS

It is important to tap into those individuals that interest you because of their story. It may be someone you ad- mire or that you find unique. Reading books should befun, but you should also want to learn more about thosewho influence your thoughts. Learn about their journeyand how they have overcome difficult times. Learn about the process and steps they had taken before they made it. Learn about how they dealt with adversities.

Think in the Now for Success

Sometimes our life's journey consists of being passion- ate about more than one thing, all of which ultimately leads us to our destiny. You may start your life wantingto be a nurse or a doctor. You may find that five years later you are interested in social work. Another fifteen years later you may be interested in becoming a Psychologist. In today's world that is normal.

It is important that you not go through that journey alone but with others. Though not all of us are blessedwith family members who can advise us, others have gained family through adopting families. By reading books, listening to motivating individuals such as pas- tors and other individuals, who you look up to plays a big role on how you "THINK IN THE NOW".

List three individuals whose life stories have captured your interest; whom you would do more research on inyour free time:

1. _____

2. _____

3. _____

Educational Investment

Commit yourself to a time, day, or month when you canstart gathering information on the individuals above. Start a journal or note taking of key qualities and/or moments in their lives that have influenced your planning and how you see yourself in the future. This process will expand your motivation, and your confidence about"your future." In addition to internal belief, studying your influencers is a great way to step into your good- ness, learning from their successes.

BE OPEN TO A NEW APPROACH

Be open to doing things differently. Be open to trying anew approach to your success. If you are an individual that often relies on what you were taught in school, you may want to learn a new approach from other sources such as your job, your close relationships, and other trusted avenues.

Most often we do not "think in the now," because we are trapped. It often reflects our known comfort zone where we live our lives based on our past. Being opento new things and new approaches is one of the most difficult life changes. However, conquering fear and not being scared to fail may be the most life-changing growth experience a person can ever have.

How Do We Become Open?
1. Get to know new people
2. Start having new conversations
3. Spend time with yourself, reflecting
4. Place your thoughts into action

CHAPTER 3

Network

Think in the Now for Success

Network

Network with a purpose. If you are at an event, personal or work purposes, you want to make continuous decisions of what individuals you are in need of in your life at that moment. For example, you may be interested in becoming an Entrepreneur. With those details, you may want to seek other Entrepreneurs to later have learning conversations and information sharing with them.

You may be interested in changing industry/interest from the medical field to business or real estate. Youmay want to target individuals that are in the field ofreal estate; an area in which you have little experience. These individuals may be able to have conversations with you that refer you to other leads, as well as help you with making a decision if the field is something in which you are truly interested (after the information and details shared).

Plan to network at least once a month or once every two months, depending on your schedule. Networking can be done at places such as:

1. Church
2. Work Related Event
3. Train, Bus or Dr.'s Office, etc.
4. Child's School

5. Personal Circle
6. Special Occasions

Networking is successful when it is planned and purposeful. If you are invited somewhere, you want to get in the mindset, in advance, of your approach, your intentions, and of course, your tools. One of the most talked about tools is business cards; however, not all of us will have a business card. If you do not have a business card, ask for others information. You can also take notes on paper temporarily and later organize appropriately.

Name three places you intend to network in the next four months:
1._____
2._____
3._____

Explain what you are expecting to gain from each event or encounter:

_____

_____

_____

_____

CHAPTER 4

Community Involvement

Community Involvement

Most likely, if you intend to be respected and successful, it is good to also be involved in molding and contributing to your community. Though most of us think involvement is about volunteering, there are other ways to be involved.

"Think for the now". You can give your ideas to help a project in environments such as your child's school, your company giving back programs, your church, and other areas that are applicable.

In addition to giving your ideas, you can be kind to your neighbors. Neighbors, not only the ones you live next to, but people you come in contact with in your everyday life. For example, helping someone at a cash register who is short a few cents to complete a transaction or helping a disabled person reach a lock or accomplish a difficult task. Also, greeting someone and sharing a smile goes a long way in a community.

Volunteering is a traditional approach to community involvement and may assist you in building your resume. Companies like to see how you operate in an environment in which you are not getting paid. It is important to see how you handle a task when money is not the only incentive.

Volunteering is also a great approach to building your skills and passion. Some individuals discover their passion from volunteer projects and involvements. In a volunteer position an individual can use the opportunity to expand on their ideas, with permission. Also in a volunteer position you test your college experience and knowledge, transferring it into productivity and sharing.

Quite often volunteer opportunities offer an individual increased confidence, hope, and a sense of appreciation and belonging. Volunteering allows us to think selflessly and to put aside our challenges for a moment and focus on helping others.

Some common Community Involvement Opportunitiesare:

1. Volunteering for an event
2. Participating on Board of Directors for a cause
3. Becoming a Member of Groups such Big BrothersBig Sisters, Affiliations such Urban Leagues, MBA Association, among other interests
4. Political Affiliations
5. Religious Affiliations
6. Other areas as per your environment

Community Involvement allows you to "live in the now" and develop relationships for tomorrow. Thereare many stories from successful individuals who received their big break through volunteering. I often ad- mire people who are willing and eager to help. In my opinion, those individuals are winners because of their

open attitude and willingness to team up. If you can bea team member, you can also be a leader.

"Remember That No Stage Is Too Small!"
Oprah Winfrey, icon

As a high school student, Winfrey entered and won the local "Miss Fire Prevention" contest. When shepicked up her prize at the local radio station, the station-master asked her if she wanted to give the mic a try. Enthralled by her voice, the station instantly hired her as a newsreader. A star was born. (Forbes Online, 1/19/2010 – forbes.com)

CHAPTER 5

Goals & Goal Setting

Think in the Now for Success

Goals and Goal Setting

As the famous Motivator and Speaker Les Brown says, "Most people fail in life not because they aim too high and miss, but because they aim too low and hit."

Setting goals does not require a vacation or two weeks off from work/school. Goal setting can be very simple. If you are an individual who struggles with following through with your plans and thoughts, then you may want to take baby steps.

Start by setting a simple goal. An example may be to sit for 5 minutes each day in silence, no televisionor other distractions. If you can accomplish a small goal, then you can accomplish bigger goals.

It is about developing the discipline. It is also about your determination to succeed and to have a healthy mind. "THINK IN THE NOW." If you can livetoday, you can make it tomorrow.

HOW DO I COME UP WITH A GOAL

What do you like about yourself? What would you like to increase about your personal strengths? You may be a great conversationalist. You may be very friendly, intuitive, or you may have skills of which only you know. A goal starts from you knowing who you areand what you would want to add to yourself to become agreater asset to society.

If you have a thought, then you can have a goal. Most individuals only set goals when under pressure and environmental situations are evident. For example, we may be pressured to buy a house, fix our credit, at- tend college, or even buy nice clothes.

There is a deeper sense of accomplishment when your intentions originate from you, and not your environment. Take a look at yourself. Do you make your own decisions? Do you "think for the now" by thinking through your next steps to your accomplishments?

TYPES OF GOALS

SHORT TERM GOALS

A short-term goal is something you want to do in the near future. The near future can mean today, this week, this month, or even this year. In other words, you may set a plan/goal to complete something for minutes from now, and you may also set a goal/plan for a year from now.

Short-term goals help us to stay in touch with our current lives and near future. When you accomplish a short-term goal, it encourages you and increases confidence in yourself to move forward to bigger things. We want to "THINK IN THE NOW."

Goals & Goal Setting

Why should I set goals?

We should set goals to remind us of our potential, our possibilities, and our skills. With goal setting, we educate ourselves about ourselves and highlight growth in:

1. What we like

2. What we are good at

3. How reliable we are

4. What we need to rearrange to succeed.

As an individual, you want to feed where you are going and not where you have been.

LONG TERM GOALS

A long-term goal is something you want to do in a year or years from the current time. The future can mean a year from now, or 20 years or so from now. Long-term goals are related to the bigger picture of your life.

Think in the Now for Success

Are Goals Changeable?

Yes, goals are changeable. As individuals, we are expected to change our minds on situations, expectations and/or life circumstances. When these elements change, we at times change our goals. Some instances are planned, and some are unexpected.

At times, you may also change your goals because you have changed your life. You may also change the direction in which you would like to go.

What are Some Common Reasons for Change?

1. Learning more about ourselves
2. Deciding that what we wanted yesterday is not what we want today.
3. The environment may change, including our jobs, the job market, our financial abilities, our location and factors affecting it, among other crucial elements.
4. Illness, health and life threatening circumstance may bring about reasons for change.
5. New knowledge:
   a. Knowledge and lessons from mentors and others you look up to.
   b. Educational investments and new insights into your future.
   c. A family decision that works for you.
   d. A change in your personal life such as your habits: Church, sports, socializing, etc.

Goals & Goal Setting

HOW TO SET A GOAL

First you want to establish what is it that you wish to accomplish. It starts with an idea, even if it is topay a bill 10 days earlier than when it is due. That is a goal. Your idea can be one of the following:

(a) to avoid interest

(b) to work on getting organized

(c) to use that time and money 10 days later for another situation or bill

(d) anything that makes you feel that you are making a difference in how you're approaching your life and your situations.

You want to document your goal or set a re- minder. It is advisable to write down your short-term goal and your long-term goals and revisit them periodically to make changes or to check them off. Documenting your thoughts/goals holds you accountable to be work on them and to be reminded of your map to success. You want to THINK IN THE NOW.

Be okay with making changes to your goals witha sense of failure and insecurity. Quite often we do notfollow through with goals, because we become discouraged about accomplishing them. We do not seem to be getting anywhere. You also want to set realistic goals that are accomplishable before you set high expectations. Setting the bar too high may remain "a thought"and not "an accomplishment.

HOW TO MEASURE YOUR GOALS

You measure your goals by staying in tune with your life and where you want to be. We often cannot determine what happens to us, but we can always deter- mine what happens within us. Your success is not the external accomplishments; however, it is also how you feel on the inside. Do you feel a sense of content? Do you feel that you at least tried something differently?

Do you feel that you learned something from the expec- tation? Would you do something differently in accom- plishing your ideas and turning them into "winners?"

You will also measure the success of your goals to the resources you have available such as:

(1)   Networking

(2)   Mandatory responsibilities

(3)   Work demands

(4)   Your state of mind

(5)   Trust in your thoughts and idea

Goals & Goal Setting

WHAT IF I STRUGGLE WITH WRITING THINGS DOWN

We all struggle at some point with taking notes of our lives and where we are trying to go. Solutions forthat may include:

a. Record your voice to a device including your phone.
b. Set a reminder on your phone or computer.
c. Have frequent meeting with others that inspire youand support you.
d. Read and spend time with self more often so that it resides with you and in you.
e. Be honest about how badly you want to THINK IN

THE NOW, how badly do you want to move forwardand succeed.

List 3 Short-Term Goals for your near future:

_____—

_____—

_____—

List 3 Long-Term Goals for your far future (past a year):

_____   —

_____   —

CHAPTER 6

Speak to YOUR Inside

Think in the Now for Success

Speak to YOUR Inside

How important do you think it is to speak to your inner self to be able to THINK IN THE NOW, to be able to be motivated? It is very important. There is a voice inside. Some of us call it faith, some call it determination, and some call it instincts.

Albert Schweitzer once said: *"In everyone's life, at some time, our inner fire goes out. It is then burst into flames by an encounter with another human being. We should all be thankful for those people who rekindle the inner spirit."*

In the previous chapters, we discussed Networking, Community Involvement, and Mentoring. Much of these add to the voice that we have inside of us. External forces, internal voice, and spirit influence a person's journey.

HOW DO I BECOME ENCOURAGED?

Sit in silence; evaluate yourself. Be true to your strengths and weaknesses. Be reminded of the thingsyou are weak for, such as your strongholds. What do I do with my weaknesses? You work on eliminating them to the best of your ability.

What do I do with my strong points and qualities? You work on increasing your strengths so they can become your CONFIDENCE AND COURAGE. It is easier said than done, yes. However, if you are determined to makea difference, succeed and to be an inspiration, you will work on increasing those qualities that you like about yourself.

Stay away from those that want to put you down, and those that are not supportive. TD Jakes once said in one of his sermons, "If you do what you have always done, then you will be where you always been." Quite often we need to break away from those things, and thosepeople that keeps us where we have always been. LIVE IN THE NOW, THINK IN THE NOW!

Napoleon Hill, "Your own emotions are yourgreatest handicap in the business of accurate thinking."

If we allow the dark parts of us to win, we lose. Wemust defeat those thoughts that say:

1. No, I cannot do this.
2. I am not good enough because I didn't acquire a degree
3. Why should they give me the job?
4. Others are better off than I am.
5. I was never good enough.

Clouding your mind with the above thoughts and emotions only blocks your POSITIVE THINKING. As most people would say, "be careful what you think, they may just become REAL." If you think positively, great things are expected to happen. It may not happen today, but remain positive and remind yourself that you are able (through previous chapter such as Goal Setting, and Educational Investment), and you will experience SUCCESS.

Your belief is bigger than your circumstances. Identify with people that have made it. THINK IN THE NOW! All positive thoughts will lead you to a better tomorrow.

"Your own emotions are your greatest handicap inthe business of accurate thinking."

~Napoleon Hill

CHAPTER 7

Give Back & Help Others

Think in the Now for Success

Give Back & Help Others

Quite often when we have found ourselves successful and more fortunate, we do not look back. It is rewarding to help others. Someone helped you along your journey. Would you not help someone?

How Can I Help Others?
1. With your ideas
2. By telling your story
3. Mentoring
4. Doing research in an area your are knowledgeable
5. Share leads and opportunities
6. Donate to a cause
7. Speak into others' lives

Others have found ways to give back by hiring and mentoring the youth. HEI (HOLISTIC EDUCATION INSTITUTE), for which I am a Co-Founder, exercises that method of giving back. Individuals have taken hands-on methods such as feeding the poor, be- cause they have been inspired by their childhood of nothaving enough food to eat. As a result, they found it very difficult to concentrate at school, and therefore, they do not want other youths to have to endure the same.

Others have taken the time out to mentor young professionals, be-friending them throughout their careers. Some professionals join forces with organizationssuch as Big Brothers, Big Sisters, Salvation Army,

And others to mentor and coach individuals. Proverbs 27:17 states, "Iron sharpeneth iron; so a man sharpeneth the countenance of his friend."

LESSONS FROM GIVING BACK & HELPINGOTHERS

1.   Quite often someone would say: "If only I knew." Helping others allows them to avoid mistakes by hearing someone else's story and experience. What better way to learn? What better way to be successful than to model someone else's journey.

2.   Often, it is difficult to give when you may not havemuch yourself. However, you may hear preachers and everyday people say, "When I give, I receive."

3.   There is something about giving that creates a warmsense of inner love and accomplishment. Giving and helping creates a better us, a HAPPIER us, and a POSI- TIVE us.

Network

What are some ways you see yourself giving back and helping others in the next 12 months?

_____ —

_____ —

_____ —

_____ —

_____ —

_____ —

_____ —

_____ —

_____ —

_____ —

_____ —

_____ —

CHAPTER 8

Treat Yourself & Reward
Yourself

Treat Yourself & Reward Yourself

While we journey through life and we live in the now, and THINK IN THE NOW, we tend to neglect our REAL selves through it all. A crucial part of growth and success is to APPRECIATE oneself.

How Do I Appreciate Myself?

Appreciating yourself may be easy for some people to do, or it may be somewhat difficult and a challenge. Many of us cheat ourselves of a great personal life because we are of the belief that money has a lot to do with appreciation. Though money contributes to appreciation, money is not necessary for you to appreciate yourself.

You can appreciate yourself by:

1.   Sitting quietly reflecting your daily accomplishments
2.   Watching one of your favorite shows
3.   Listening to your favorite Speaker, Author, Artist,etc.
4.   Watching a show that is outside of your comfortzone, meant for laughter or as a stress reliever
5.   Treating yourself to a great walk in the park or anouting in the community
6.   Documenting in a journal your thoughts and experiences
7.   Updating and rearranging your goals can give asense of appreciation for your TRUTH

8. Admitting your strengths and deciding how to in-crease them

9. Pampering yourself physically (hair, nails, facial, ameal) at home

10. Building your drive, perseverance, and tenacity...

TALK TO YOURSELF, be your biggest support!

As John Maxwell shared in one of his presentations, "Most accomplishments in life come more easily if you approach them strategically." In other words, by spending time with yourself, you are able to THINK in depth which may lead to strategies. Most successful people do not wake up one day and find themselves successful, overnight. You have to work for it; you have to want it badly. When you want something badly, you will develop the mind for it. How will you do that?

Through your thinking, through your quiet time with yourself, and by talking to yourself. Your answers will be your thoughts, your ideas; these will becomeyour realities. Your accomplishments are birthed or created from the appreciation you have for yourself. If you appreciate yourself, you will appreciate your thoughtsthat may become your realities (accomplishment/ success). Positive thinking leads to reality. If you can think it, YOU can be.

Reflect on the quote mentioned in an earlier chapter, "If you always do what you have always done, then you will be where you have always been."

Treat Yourself & Reward Yourself

You Can Reward Yourself By:

1. Buying used books
2. Researching and checking the best deal for your rewards (this may take weeks or months at a time)
3. Cheating and buying chocolate or ice cream as a reward occasionally
4. Preparing a healthy meal or a healthy smoothie withfruits or vegetables
5. Taking a day off from strategic thinking and goalsetting
6. Planning a vacation to a place you have never been
7. Checking off your accomplishments from yourvision board, goals, plans, etc.
8. Setting money aside to spend at the Mall on something you always wanted but could not afford, or that was not a necessity
9. Signing up for a seminar or network event that is in alignment with YOUR NEW INTEREST
10. Keep on keeping on FEEL good about your journey

Reward is similar to Appreciation.

Appreciation: *Recognition of the quality, value, sig-nificance, or magnitude of people and things.*

Reward: *A thing given in recognition of one's service, effort, or achievement.*

Think in the Now for Success

Appreciating one's self does not require much investment financially. It can be your way of recognizing yourself and thanking yourself with small gestures of GRATEFULNESS. It starts from the little things that we do to motivate and thank ourselves that leads to the bigger gestures.

Rewarding one's self, on the other hand, may in- volve giving yourself something. This gesture may in- volve memorable actions such as listed above and others. A reward has more thoughts and purposeful actions invested.

List examples of how you intend to appreciate yourselfand reward yourself in the next week of your journey:

_____ —

_____ —

_____ —

_____ —

_____ —

_____ —

_____ —

CHAPTER 9

Think in the Now for Success

Think in the Now for Success

I recall when I made a list of my "To Do" list, my long-term goals. I named the list "ON THE WAY." On that list, I included four huge, meaningful goals. At times, individuals have numerous names for their lists. Some familiar names are (1) goals, (2) vision board, (3) my "To Do" list, or simply (4) my thoughts. It goes back to one of my favorite quotes, "If you can believe it you can see it, if you can visualize it, it can happen."

Before I came up with a list, I started with my ideas and my thoughts. I took in motion thinking in the now. What can I think of today that I wish to become a reality and how will I get there? I included on the list:
(1) Become a Notary Public, (2) Motivational Speaker/Empowerment Expert, (3) Coach and Trainer, and (4) Author.

I made the list two years ago. When I created the list on a white board that I purchased from the famous Dollar Tree Store, I had no idea that it would come to FRUITION. After making my list colorful, attractive and complete, I made an important move. What did I do? I then took that white board and placed it on theside of my refrigerator that I visit multiple times a day. My plan was to read it as often as possible. My planwas to be familiar with my thoughts and desires; that would later become my goals and dreams that would later become my SUCCESSES.

Think in the Now for Success

To date, all of those goals have been accomplished, including becoming an Author by writing this very book you are reading. The most rewarding experience of that journey was that I did not create worry nor was I concerned about HOW I would accomplish those goals. My approach was to think it IF I CAN THINK IT; I CAN ACHIEVE IT.

I want to invite you deeper into this experience. After I had the thought that I wanted to become an Author, I had no idea what the book would be about, neither did I have a clue of the title.

One day it came to me clear as day, the title of this book will be "THINK IN THE NOW." Again, I had no idea of all the details, but I took action to my THOUGHT.

Two days later, before it left my thoughts, I wrote the title that came to me on a sticky note, in bright colors. What did I do with that sticky note? I fastened the note, with tape on my door, from the inside. I decided that I wanted see the name all the time, to remind me of my thinking, my goals, and my journey.

Why did I want to see the name? If I can see it, I can believe it. If I can believe it, I can see it. If I can believe it, I can achieve it. I saw that title for months. Day after day. While I saw the title as I entered and exited the home, I refused to worry or exhaust myself about the next step. Why? It will come to you if you let it. THINK IN THE NOW.

Think in the Now for Success

I was thinking in the now, and everything else followed.

Six months later, I decided it was time to writethe contents of the book. Then, and only then I foundthe need to take it to another level. If you find a "THINKING SPACE," and "THINKING TIME" you
would be amazed at the thoughts that would come your way. Most of the inventions that exist were first a THOUGHT in the inventor's mind. Stick to your ideas, do not give up and rush the time. You would be amazed of how THOSE IDEAS translate into money, a success- ful job, a certification, an opportunity to increase, great rewarding business relationships, and so much more.

In Conclusion

THINKING IN THE NOW FOR SUCCESS causes us to reflect on many of our everyday experiences. Much of our past approaches to situations and circumstances affect how we THINK IN THE NOW. As individuals, we can use those past experiences and approaches to positively affect how we move forward and think today for tomorrow. The educational investment you make in yourself on a DAILY basis is what counts for tomorrow. A college education is exceptional; however EDUCATION is also from our EVERYDAY THINKING and EVERYDAY LEARNING.

It is crucial to utilize the power we have inside of us. Talk to your inside! THINK IN THE NOW for what you know will become a reality. YOU are your biggest and BEST motivator.

Do not forget to give back. The same way some- one believed in you and inspired you is the same way you can give back to a person or cause.

Set goals and expectations for yourself. THINK IN THE NOW for your success and achievements. If you can think it, it can become a reality. Appreciate yourself, at every moment and every instance you can. People will treat you, in the manner you treat yourself(it is a reflection); you are a "walking example" of your- self.

"Feed where you are going, and not where you have been!"

THINK IN THE NOW; LIVE IN THE NOW.

Bibliography

Senior Consultant, Entrepreneur & Small Business Consultant, Author, Career & Job Performance Coach, Training & Development Expert, Strategist, Isidora Izzy Lewis is the Owner of Feel Better-Do Better Staffing Both entities serve a community-based movement with a mission to maximize potential in individuals. It wasthe perseverance of "daring to be different" in 1973 at a young age that birthed this humble and serving leader and company she co- founded.

Izzy Lewis, born Isidora Yvette Lewis to the proud parents Percy Lewis, Sr. and Florine Lewis. Izzy, as the youngest of her medium size family, developed her leadership and negotiation skills very early in her life, by negotiating with her siblings and parents. From a tenderyoung age, Izzy was determined to embrace her uniqueness and her assertive goal-getting personality. At age 21 she attained a Bachelor'sDegree, which was the first major step towards her business and careerbreakthrough.

Over the years she has worked with major companies such Columbia University in the City of New York, and community-based organizations such as The Salvation Army. Izzy takes pride in education and everyday learning and has attained degrees and certificates from various universities, her most recent being Southern Methodist University in Dallas TX. She is the Author of articles listed as "Giving Minds Their Wings", "A Look At Your Life, Where It Is," and "Being Multi-Talented May Not Be As Recognized."

Izzy continues to embrace her devotion/patriotism by her many contributions to the community; listed as work with NPOs, development of the Youth through Interactive Workshops, Mentoring, as an Adjunct Professor, and Coach/Mediator. Izzy takes pride in her involvements such as Small Business and Entrepreneur MeetUp Group, serving on the Career Services Advisory Committee of North Lake College (DCCCD Community Colleges), The Mentor Matcher Board of Directors, as well as servicing the community as a Notary.

Ms. Lewis looks forward to maximizing potential and sharingand developing our community, through her recent endeavor as the author of *THINK IN THE NOW FOR SUCCESS.*

Feel Better - Do Better Staffing & Consulting
Maximizing Potential